# CA$H OUT
# PROPERTY

## JOSH CUNNINGHAM

KEY PERSON INFLUENCE
SHARK TANK

"
Josh Cunningham's reputation in real estate is unparalleled. His strategies and insights are invaluable for anyone in the market.

KEVIN HARRINGTON

Original Shark on the Hit TV Show, "Shark Tank"
Inventor of the Infomercial ($5 Billion in Global Sales)
"One of the top entrepreneurs of our time!" -
Entrepreneur Magazine

Josh is a leader who serves others! He will inspire you with Championship ideas that are essential for winning in business and life!

JOE THEISMANN

Legendary NFL Super Bowl Champion Quarterback
12 Year NFL Veteran, Winner of NFL MVP & NFL Man of the Year
Football TV Commentator, ESPN & NFL Network

JAMES
MALINCHAK
FEATURED ON THE HIT ABC TV SHOW
SECRET MILLIONAIRE

> What I love about Josh's book is that he takes things one step further than most other authors.  And this step is ultra important.  He not only presents the problems - known and unknown - that you will see in the real estate world but he actually provides solutions to those challenges you will face.  And he does this in such a way that it is easily understandable and immediately actionable.  This is a must read.

## KEVIN EASTMAN

Former NBA Championship Coach with Boston Celtics
Current Corporate & Sports Team Speaker
www.kevineastman.net

> **Josh shows you how to get maximum value and cash out of your property, quickly and efficiently, and hassle free**

## BRIAN TRACY

President - Brian Tracy International

Top Selling Author of Over 70 books

Has Addressed more than 5,000,000 people in 5,000 talks and seminars throughout the US, Canada & 77 other countries worldwide

**"Josh's strategies are a beacon of hope for anyone facing real estate woes. He's not just an expert; he's a lifesaver."**

## JILL LUBIN

Media Magnet, 4x Best Selling Author, International Speaker
www.JillLubin.com

" **This book is the secret weapon and blueprint that every person and professional who has property and needs some immediate options to achieve their financial goals. Josh Cunningham has put together a unique collection of life's lessons and personal wealth success strategies to help you thrive and succeed with your property. His book is incredibly noteworthy, extremely valuable, and inspiring to help you have a plan to increase wealth, overcome any challenges and be better to grow successfully. "Cash Out Property" is a must read and truly magical!  Well done!** "

**JOHN FORMICA**

The "Ex-Disney Guy"
America's Customer Experience Coach at www.JohnFormica.com

**"Josh Cunningham is a person who inspires and leads others!  His ideas are proven for producing results!  Josh is on a mission to make a positive difference in the lives of others!"**

## PATTY AUBERY

#1 NY Times Best-Selling Author, Chicken Soup for the Christian Soul
Former President, Chicken Soup for the Soul
Current President, Jack Canfield Companies

# SPECIAL FREE BONUS
# GIFT FOR YOU

**Free Consultation Invitation for" Real Estate Solutions with Josh Cunningham"**

**Discover Your Property's Potential:** Free, No-Obligation Consultation

**You're Not Alone in This Journey**

Navigating the complexities of real estate can be overwhelming, especially when faced with personal challenges or unique property situations. Whether you're dealing with financial distress, managing an inherited property, or simply seeking a quick and hassle-free sale, I understand the myriad of emotions and decisions you're grappling with.

**Tailored Solutions, Just for You**

Each property, like its owner, has a unique story. That's why I offer personalized consultations, free of charge and without obligation. In our one-on-one session, we'll explore your specific situation, address your concerns, and evaluate your property's potential. You'll gain insights into the current market and learn what your home could truly be worth.

**Why Choose Josh Cunningham?**

- **20+ Years of Diverse Real Estate Experience:** From investing to property management, I've seen it all.

- **Win-Win Philosophy:** My commitment is to find solutions that benefit everyone involved.

- **Proven Track Record:** Trusted by top real estate owners across the U.S. and Canada.

- **Solution-Oriented Approach:** No matter how complex your situation, I am dedicated to finding the best outcome for you.

**Your Next Step**

Ready to discover what your home could be worth and explore your options? Schedule your free consultation today. Let's find the right solution together, with no pressure and no strings attached.

*Your property has potential. Let's unlock it together.*

**Contact Information**

- Phone Number: 832-819-5496

- Email Address: josh@CashOutProperty.com

- Website: www.CashOutProperty.com

# INSPIRING CHANGE THROUGH WORDS:
## JOSH CUNNINGHAM ON STAGE

Empowering Audiences in Entrepreneurship and Beyond

As a seasoned real estate expert and an influential voice in the business world, I, Josh Cunningham, take my wealth of knowledge beyond the pages of this book and onto stages across the nation. Speaking on a variety of critical topics, my goal is to ignite passion, drive change, and provide valuable insights in areas including:

- **Entrepreneurship:** Sharing the roadmap to building successful ventures, drawing from my own journey and lessons learned.

- **Sales Mastery:** Unveiling strategies that have transformed my approach to sales, guaranteeing not just transactions, but lasting relationships.

- **Exceptional Customer Service:** Discussing the art of exceeding customer expectations to create brand ambassadors for life.

- **Building Company Culture:** Revealing the keys to fostering a company culture that motivates, retains, and nurtures talent.

- **Hiring & Training Excellence:** Offering insights into finding and cultivating the best talent, the cornerstone of any successful business.

## Connect with Me – Stay Informed and Inspired

Staying connected means staying empowered. Follow me on social media for regular updates, tips, and insights. It's not just about staying informed; it's about being part of a community that values growth and excellence in business.

- https://www.linkedin.com/in/cultureisthekey

- https://twitter.com/cultureisthekey

- https://www.facebook.com/cultureisthekey

- https://www.instagram.com/cultureisthekey

- https://www.tiktok.com/@cultureisthekey

- https://www.youtube.com/@cultureisthekey

## Catch Me Live: Upcoming Speaking Engagements

There's a unique energy and insight that comes from a live event, and I'd love for you to be part of it. Visit my website for a calendar of my upcoming speaking engagements and find out where you can join me next. Let's connect, learn, and grow together.

- Website for Event Schedule: www.fivestarcompanyculture.com

# CONGRATULATIONS

Thank you for picking up this book. As you embark on these pages, you're taking an important step toward understanding the complexities and opportunities in real estate, especially in challenging circumstances.

This guide is designed to offer you insight, understanding, and practical solutions. Whether you're navigating personal hurdles with your property, seeking to optimize your real estate investments, or simply exploring your options, you'll find valuable knowledge here.

My aim is to provide you with both the information and the inspiration you need to make informed decisions. With real-life examples, straightforward advice, and a focus on empathetic solutions, I hope to empower you in your real estate journey.

Happy reading, and here's to discovering the potential in every property and situation!

**-Josh Cunningham**
Founder, www.CashOutProperty.com

# DEDICATION

*To My Beloved Family,*

*This book is dedicated to you, the unwavering pillars of my life. Your love, support, and belief in me have been the foundation upon which I've built not only my career but my entire being.*

*To my wonderful wife, Faith, thank you for being my rock, my partner, and my constant source of inspiration. Your strength, wisdom, and compassion light up my world, guiding me through every challenge and celebrating every triumph.*

*To my precious children, Ellie and Griffin, you are my greatest achievements. Watching you grow, laugh, and explore the world fills my heart with indescribable joy. You remind me daily of what truly matters and inspire me to be the best version of myself.*

*To my parents, Brad and Cathy, thank you for always believing in me and supporting my dreams, no matter how big or far-fetched they seemed. Your endless encouragement and love have shaped the person I am today. I am forever grateful for the sacrifices you've made and the lessons you've taught me.*

*This journey would not have been the same without each of you. You are my motivation, my support system, and my reason for striving to make a difference in the world.*

*With all my love,*

**Josh, aka Dada**

# TABLE OF
# CONTENTS

*Chapter: 1*

# INTRODUCTION

## Understanding Your Situation

Life has its unexpected turns. Whether it's a sudden job relocation, a financial bind, an inherited property you're not prepared to manage, or any number of personal emergencies, the need to sell your property quickly and without hassle can be a pressing concern. This is where your journey begins, and where we step in.

In the world of real estate transactions, especially under pressing circumstances, the path isn't always clear. The traditional process of selling a home can be daunting, time-consuming, and laden with uncertainties. This is particularly true if you're dealing with a property that's seen better days or you're navigating a complex personal situation.

But what if there were better, more streamlined options? What if you could find a solution that not only eases your immediate burden but also provides a fair, efficient, and stress-free transaction?

## The Journey to a Solution

That's where I, Josh Cunningham, come into the picture. With 20+ years of experience in real estate investment, property management, and sales, I've dedicated my career to creating win-win situations for people just like you. I've worked with hundreds of top real estate agents and teams across the United States and Canada, managing millions of online leads, and training over 400 sales professionals. But the core of my work has always been about solving problems — your problems.

This book is more than just a guide; it's a pathway to understanding your options and making informed decisions. You might feel cornered by your current circumstances, but there are more choices available to you than you might realize.

In the following chapters, we'll explore these options. From a fast sale for cash, leveraging a vast network of investors for a better deal, innovative financing solutions, to the more traditional routes — each has its unique benefits tailored to different needs and situations. My commitment is to help you find the solution that best fits your life, your property, and your goals.

As you turn the pages, keep in mind that every situation is unique and deserves a personalized approach. I invite you to journey through these options with an open mind. The stories and strategies shared here are drawn from real experiences and tailored to address real challenges. Whether you're a seasoned property owner or new to the world of real estate, you'll find valuable insights and practical advice.

As we embark on this journey together, remember that my ultimate goal is to provide you with a solution that not only resolves your immediate needs but also leaves you in a better position than when we started. Your peace of mind, your financial well-being, and your future are at the heart of what I do.

And while this book is a comprehensive resource, it's just the beginning. I'm here to engage in a conversation, to listen to your story, and to work alongside you in finding the best path forward. So, as you read, I encourage you to jot down questions, make notes of your specific circumstances, and consider how the solutions presented might align with your needs.

In the next chapter, we'll dive into the common challenges and pain points you might be facing. Understanding these is the first step in navigating towards a solution. Together, we'll explore these challenges not just as obstacles, but as opportunities to move forward in a positive, productive way.

*Chapter: 2*

# UNDERSTANDING DISTRESS: YOUR PAIN POINTS

In the world of real estate, each property tells a story, and so does every seller. The reasons behind the need to sell a property are as varied as life itself. In this chapter, we'll explore common situations that bring homeowners and property owners to the point of sale – often under less-than-ideal circumstances. Understanding these scenarios is the first step in finding the right solution.

## Personal Emergencies and Financial Distress

Financial crises can strike unexpectedly, leaving homeowners in a precarious position. The stress of looming debts, compounded by the need for a quick resolution, can make traditional property selling methods seem inadequate.

Example: John's job loss led to a financial spiral, culminating in a foreclosure threat. His situation needed a solution that was not only swift but also sensitive to his immediate financial challenges.

## Challenges of Distressed Properties

Owning a property that requires significant repairs can feel like a constant battle. These properties pose a dilemma: invest heavily in renovations or try to sell as-is in a market that favors pristine homes.

Example: Sarah's inherited family home, laden with memories, also came with the burden of disrepair. Faced with the daunting task of extensive renovations, she sought an alternative route to avoid the traditional, costly selling process.

## Elderly Downsizing

For many seniors, there comes a time when a large family home is no longer practical or desirable. The emotional and physical challenges of downsizing, coupled with the need for a timely sale, require a sensitive and efficient approach.

**Example:** Martha, moving to a senior living community, faced the emotional task of selling her home of many years. Quick and compassionate handling of the sale was essential for her peace of mind and smooth transition.

## Financial Overextension

Changes in financial circumstances, such as interest rate increases or income loss, can turn a manageable mortgage into an unbearable burden. The rapid sale of the property often becomes the most viable option to prevent further financial downfall.

**Example:** David and Lisa's dream home became a financial nightmare when interest rates surged. To prevent falling deeper into debt, they needed a quick and reliable way to sell their home.

## Environmental Issues

Environmental problems in a property, whether due to natural disasters or long-term neglect, create unique challenges in the real estate market. These properties require a seller who can navigate these complexities with expertise.

Example: After a flood, Jack's home developed severe mold issues, making it unsellable through traditional avenues. He needed a solution that could handle these environmental challenges without the burden of personal investment.

## The Landlord's Dilemma

The challenges of being a landlord – from uncooperative tenants to constant maintenance – can turn a profitable investment sour. For landlords at their wits' end, selling the property often becomes the most appealing solution.

Example: Mr. and Mrs. Anderson's rental property, once a source of income, had become a source of endless stress due to tenant issues and ongoing repairs. A straightforward sale was their best option to move on from these challenges.

## Inherited Properties: A Sudden Responsibility

Inheriting a property can be overwhelming, especially if it comes with liabilities or maintenance needs. The emotional and logistical aspects of selling such a property often necessitate a unique selling approach.

**Example:** Alex, who inherited a property in a different state, was unprepared to become a long-distance landlord or deal with the selling process remotely. He required a solution that could manage these unique circumstances efficiently.

## Divorce and Asset Liquidation

Divorce often brings the difficult task of dividing assets, including property. In such emotionally charged situations, a fair, quick, and straightforward property sale is essential to move forward.

**Example:** Ashley and Tom, navigating a divorce, needed to sell their joint property swiftly and without added emotional strain, highlighting the need for a straightforward and empathetic selling process.

## Vacant Properties

Vacant properties, while seemingly harmless, can become financial drains due to maintenance costs, vandalism, and other issues. For owners, selling such properties quickly can prevent further losses and liabilities.

**Example:** Kevin's inherited vacant property quickly became a target for vandalism, turning what was once an asset into a liability. He sought a solution to sell this property promptly, avoiding the ongoing issues and costs associated with vacancy.

## Code Violations and Legal Issues

Properties with legal complications, such as unresolved code violations or liens, present unique challenges in the selling process. These issues often require specialized knowledge and handling for a successful sale.

**Example:** Debbie discovered her inherited property had numerous code violations, making a traditional sale almost impossible. She needed a selling approach that could navigate these legal complexities effectively.

## Chapter Summary

In this chapter, we've explored a range of scenarios that lead homeowners and property owners to consider selling under distressing circumstances. From the financial pressures of job loss and foreclosure to the physical and emotional challenges of maintaining a distressed or inherited property, each situation presents its own set of difficulties. Landlord struggles, environmental issues, legal complications, and the emotional turmoil of life changes like divorce or downsizing in later life further illustrate the diverse challenges in the real estate market.

These stories represent just a fraction of the myriad situations you might be facing. Understanding these challenges is the first step towards finding a solution that respects your needs and provides a way forward. As we move into the next chapters, we'll look at how these challenges can be met with effective, empathetic solutions tailored to your unique situation. You're not alone in this journey, and there are options available to navigate these trying times with dignity and hope.

*Chapter: 3*

# SOLUTIONS FOR YOUR UNIQUE NEEDS

The following chapters of the book offer a comprehensive guide to the various solutions available for homeowners looking to sell their properties under different circumstances. Each section is tailored to address specific scenarios, ensuring homeowners find the most suitable option for their needs.

**Fast Sale for Cash:** This chapter details the process of a quick sale for immediate cash. It's ideal for those needing an urgent sale due to financial distress or personal emergencies. The benefits include a fast and hassle-free transaction with minimal paperwork.

**Accessing Our Nationwide Network of Investors:** For those seeking potentially higher returns, this part explores leveraging a network of investors. It explains how this approach can unlock more lucrative opportunities compared to a standard sale.

**Creative Financing Solutions:** This segment covers innovative financial solutions for unique selling situations. It's designed for sellers looking for tailored options beyond traditional sales methods, providing flexibility in terms of financing and deal structuring.

**The Traditional Listing Approach:** The most detailed and comprehensive section, it guides sellers through the traditional real estate listing process. It's the most time-consuming option but often yields the highest return. Key steps include property preparation, strategic marketing, effective negotiations, and navigating the complexities of closing the deal.

The content of each section is structured to be direct and informative, steering clear of unnecessary complexity. The focus remains on providing clear, actionable information, underscored by practical insights drawn from extensive real estate experience. This approach ensures that you are equipped with the knowledge needed to navigate your selling journey confidently, aligned with your specific needs and goals.

*Chapter: 4*

# FAST SALE FOR CASH

In times of distress, the need for a quick, uncomplicated property sale becomes paramount. A fast sale for cash is a solution designed to meet this need, offering a streamlined process free from the usual complexities of traditional real estate transactions. This option is especially suitable if you're looking to sell your property swiftly without the hassle of repairs, staging, or enduring the uncertainties of the market.

## The Quick and Hassle-Free Process

The process of a fast cash sale is straightforward. It begins with a simple assessment of your property, followed by a fair cash offer. This offer is based on the current market conditions and the state of your property, ensuring transparency and fairness. Unlike conventional sales, this process doesn't involve multiple showings, staging, or waiting for buyer financing approvals.

Once you accept the offer, the closing can be arranged in as little as two weeks, a stark contrast to the months it often takes in a traditional sale. This expedited timeline is ideal if you're dealing with time-sensitive situations like impending foreclosure, a quick relocation, or simply the desire to close a chapter swiftly and start anew.

**Key Benefits of a Fast Cash Sale:**

+ **THE CERTAINTY OF THE SALE:** In a typical market, even after accepting an offer, sales can fall through due to financing issues or failed inspections. A cash sale removes these uncertainties, providing you with a guaranteed sale and peace of mind.

+ **PRIVACY AND DISCRETION NOT ALWAYS FOUND IN TRADITIONAL SALES:** Your property won't be listed publicly for months, and the sale details remain confidential, allowing you to move forward with your life without unnecessary public scrutiny.

+ **NO FEES OR COMMISSIONS:** One of the most significant benefits is the absence of realtor fees or commissions. This means more of the sale proceeds go directly to you, the seller, without deductions often encountered in traditional sales.

+ **NO CLOSING COSTS – 100% FREE:** The transaction doesn't involve typical closing costs. The investor handles all associated expenses, making the process entirely free for you.

+ **NO HOME REPAIRS NEEDED:** You won't need to invest in repairs or renovations. The property is purchased 'as-is,' saving you the time, money, and effort that would otherwise go into making your property market-ready.

+ **FAST AND FAIR OFFERS:** Offers are made quickly and are based on a fair assessment of your property's value in its current condition, ensuring transparency and fairness in the deal.

+ **YOU SET THE CONDITIONS:** You have the flexibility to set the terms that work best for your situation, whether it's the closing timeline or other specific needs, providing you with control over the sale process.

## Understanding Investor Risks in Fast Cash Sales

While a fast sale for cash offers numerous benefits to you as the seller, it's also important to recognize the risks and responsibilities undertaken by the investor in this process. This understanding underscores the value of the service provided and the expertise required to manage these risks effectively.

**Funding the Purchase:** Investors need to have substantial capital available to fund the purchase of your property. This capital is often sourced from personal funds, investment groups, or through financial loans, each carrying its own risks and costs.

**Managing Repairs and Renovations:** Post-purchase, the investor is responsible for all repairs and renovations needed to make the property marketable. This involves not just a financial investment but also the challenges of working with contractors, managing timelines, and ensuring quality work.

**Market Volatility Risks:** The real estate market is subject to fluctuations and changes. Investors take on the risk of market volatility; if the market declines between the purchase and resale, they face the potential for financial loss.

**Regulatory and Compliance Responsibilities:** Investors need to stay abreast of and comply with various regulations, building codes, and legal requirements. Non-compliance can lead to legal issues and financial penalties.

**Occupancy Challenges:** If the property is occupied, whether by tenants or the previous owners, the investor must manage the process of ensuring the property is vacated, which can sometimes involve legal proceedings.

These risks taken on by the investor in a fast cash sale scenario are significant and require a blend of financial acumen, market knowledge, and operational expertise. They represent the behind-the-scenes complexities that enable you, the seller, to enjoy a hassle-free, quick sale process.

## Calculating a Fair Offer

To ensure transparency and fairness in our cash offers, we follow a straightforward formula. It begins with the ARV (After Repair Value), which is our estimate of what your home will sell for after necessary renovations. From this value, we deduct the estimated cost of those renovations – our Repair Budget. Next, we account for the Costs to Resell, which include agent fees typically ranging from 6-7%, closing costs like title and escrow fees at about 1-2%, and other taxes, totaling approximately 10% of the ARV. We also subtract our Profit, an essential aspect of our business model, generally around 10% of the ARV. The final figure, after these deductions, is Your Cash Offer. This is the amount we can pay you for your home, with the flexibility of choosing your closing date. This offer is transparent, with no hidden fees or commissions – the number you see is exactly what you receive for your house.

| ARV | After Repair value. This is what we expect the home to sell for after we've fixed it up. |
| --- | --- |
| **- Repair Budget** | This is how much we estimate the renovation to cost us. |
| **- Costs to Resell** | Unfortunately, when we resell, we have to pay agent fees. Typical real estate commissions are 6-7% and closing costs (title and escrow fees) are another 1-2% and other taxes can be roughly 1-2%. We expect this to wind up around 10%. |
| **- Profit** | Don't let our transparency surprise you, we wouldn't be able to remain operational without turning a profit. Our profit is usually around 10% of the selling price (ARV) |
| **Your Cash Offer** | This is how much we can give you for your home on the closing date of your choice. No hidden fees, commissions or anything. This number is exactly how much we pay your for your house. |

## Chapter Summary:

The 'Fast Sale for Cash' option is a streamlined, efficient solution for homeowners looking to sell their properties quickly and without the usual complexities of traditional real estate transactions. This approach is particularly beneficial for those facing urgent circumstances like foreclosure, relocation, or simply desiring a rapid sale without the hassles of a conventional process.

This cash offer option is designed to provide you with a stress-free, efficient, and fair way to sell your property, catering to your unique needs and circumstances.

*Chapter: 5*

# ACCESSING OUR NATIONWIDE NETWORK OF INVESTORS

## Leveraging Connections for Your Benefit

In the dynamic world of real estate, having a robust network can be a game changer. This is where my extensive network of nationwide investors comes into play, offering a unique solution for property sellers like you. This approach is particularly beneficial for those who are seeking alternatives beyond a simple cash sale or traditional market listing. Let's dive into how this network operates and why it can be an advantageous route for you.

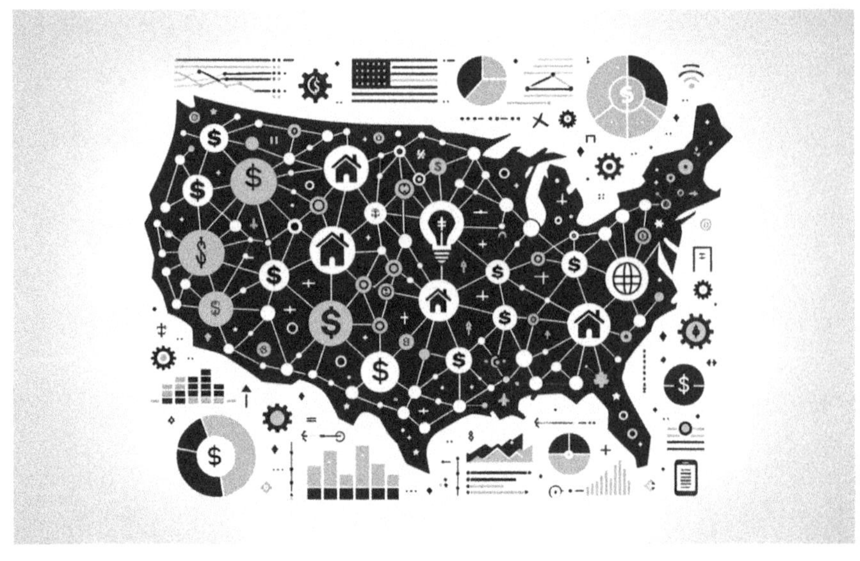

## Why Choose Our Investor Network?

+ **Expanded Opportunities:** Our network encompasses a diverse range of investors, each looking for different types of properties. Whether your property is a fixer-upper, a rental, or something unique, there's likely an investor interested in what you have.

+ **Competitive Offers:** Investors in our network understand the value of real estate and are often prepared to make competitive offers. This can sometimes lead to better financial outcomes than traditional sales methods.

+ **Flexibility in Transactions:** Investors often have the ability to be more flexible in their deals. This can include various purchasing arrangements, quicker closing times, and sometimes even creative financing options.

## How It Works

The process begins with a comprehensive evaluation of your property. We consider factors like location, condition, and current market trends. This assessment helps in matching your property with the right investors from our network.

- **Property Evaluation:** We start with a thorough assessment of your property to understand its potential value and appeal to investors.

- **Matching with Investors:** Based on the evaluation, we identify potential investors from our network who are looking for properties like yours.

- **Negotiation and Offers:** We facilitate the negotiation process, aiming to secure an offer that aligns with your goals and expectations.

- **Closing the Deal:** Once an agreement is reached, we ensure a smooth closing process, handling all necessary paperwork and coordination.

## The Potential for a Better Return

Utilizing our investor network can open doors to opportunities that might not be available through traditional selling methods. Investors often look for properties they can add value to, which means they might be interested in properties that don't appeal to typical homebuyers. This interest can translate into a better return for you, the seller.

+ **Value-Add Potential:** Investors are often looking for properties where they can add value, which might make your property more appealing to them than to the average buyer.

+ **Less Hassle, More Gain:** Selling to an investor can be a simpler, more straightforward process. This can mean fewer showings, no need for repairs or staging, and a faster closing.

## Chapter Summary:

Tapping into our nationwide network of investors presents a unique and potentially lucrative route for selling your property. This approach is especially useful for those who seek a swift, hassle-free sale with the potential for a competitive return. Our role is to bridge the gap between your property and these investors, ensuring a seamless and beneficial transaction for all parties involved.

*Chapter: 6*

# CREATIVE FINANCING SOLUTIONS

## Innovative Approaches to Traditional Problems

Navigating the complexities of real estate transactions can be daunting, especially when traditional methods don't align with your needs or objectives. Creative financing solutions step in to fill this gap, offering flexibility and innovation. Here, the focus is not solely on immediate cash transactions but on structuring deals that can meet your financial goals under varied circumstances.

## Tailoring the Deal to Your Needs

Creative financing is about customizing the terms of a real estate transaction to benefit all parties involved. It's particularly useful when you, as a seller, are aiming to get your desired price but are open to flexibility in other aspects of the deal. We will explore two key creative financing strategies:

**#1 Owner Financing:** This is a powerful tool for sellers looking to achieve their desired sale price. In owner financing, you provide the buyer with a loan to purchase the property. By being flexible with the terms of the loan, such as the down payment, interest rate, and amortization period, you can negotiate a deal that meets your financial objectives while making the property accessible to the buyer.

- **Down Payment Flexibility:** You might accept a lower initial down payment, making the property more accessible to a wider range of buyers, potentially leading to a quicker sale.

- **Interest Rate Negotiation:** Setting an interest rate that is competitive yet favorable can be more profitable in the long term compared to a straight cash sale.

- **Amortization Period:** Offering longer amortization periods can reduce the monthly payment burden on the buyer, making it easier to agree on a higher sale price.

In the dynamic world of real estate investing, the decision between "becoming the bank" through owner financing and being a traditional landlord represents two fundamentally different paths. While both strategies have their unique benefits, many investors are discovering that "becoming the bank" offers distinct advantages. This approach shifts the focus from property management to financial management, aligning more with a lender's role. Below, we explore the key reasons why this strategy is often viewed as a more advantageous and streamlined approach to real estate investment.

- **Steady, Predictable Income:** Owner financing provides a consistent stream of income through monthly payments from the buyer. Unlike rental income, which can fluctuate due to vacancies or unexpected repairs, the income from owner financing is more stable and predictable.

+ **Lower Management Responsibilities:** As the lender, you're not responsible for the day-to-day upkeep of the property. This means no late-night calls about broken plumbing, no dealing with tenant disputes, and no property maintenance tasks. Your role is primarily financial, significantly reducing the time and effort spent on property management.

+ **Reduced Risk:** In owner financing, the buyer assumes responsibility for the property, including maintenance and repairs. This shift reduces your risk of property damage and the associated costs. Additionally, you avoid the common landlord challenges like tenant turnover, eviction processes, and property wear and tear.

+ **Tax Advantages:** Spreading out the receipt of the property's sale price over several years can potentially offer favorable tax implications. This might include deferring some capital gains taxes, as opposed to a lump-sum sale where taxes are due all at once.

+ **Broader Market Appeal:** Offering owner financing can attract a wider pool of potential buyers. This can be particularly beneficial in selling properties that are unique or situated in slower real estate markets.

In summary, owner financing is a compelling option for those seeking a more hands-off investment with steady cash flow, fewer management headaches, and lower risk compared to traditional landlord responsibilities. It appeals to investors looking for a simpler, more predictable path in real estate.

**#2 Subject-To Deals:** In a subject-to transaction, the buyer takes over the property payments, but the mortgage remains in your name. This strategy can be particularly useful if you're looking to sell quickly. You can negotiate the terms of the sale to reflect the price you desire, while providing a manageable pathway for the buyer to assume control of the property. The flexibility in such deals can be around how much the buyer pays upfront and how they plan to refinance the property in the future to eventually remove the mortgage from your name.

A frequent concern for sellers considering subject-to deals is how retaining their existing mortgage, while moving to a new property, might impact their debt-to-income (DTI) ratio. This concern is particularly valid for those looking to purchase a new property but are encumbered by an existing mortgage that they can't offload without incurring financial loss.

## Solution: Addressing the Debt-to-Income Ratio Concern

**Educating the Seller:** It's crucial to understand that loan officers are not the ultimate decision-makers in the lending process; underwriters are. Therefore, direct communication with underwriters is essential to address this specific concern effectively.

**Lease Agreement Strategy:**

- Creating a Lease Agreement: One effective strategy is to draft a lease agreement, showing that the investor (who is buying the property subject-to) will lease the seller's property.

- Upfront Payments: Making two payments upfront can demonstrate the investor's commitment and financial stability.

- Flexible Lease Structure: The agreement can be structured to allow the investor to cancel the lease at any point, providing additional flexibility.

**Effect on Debt-to-Income Ratio:**

- By establishing a lease agreement and making upfront payments, it's possible to persuade the underwriter to exclude the existing mortgage payments from the seller's DTI calculation.

- This adjustment can significantly aid the seller in qualifying for a new loan for their next property.

**Using a Licensed Loan Servicing Company:**

- For a more long-term and sustainable solution, employing a licensed loan servicing company to manage the subject-to loan payments is advisable.

- This approach offers documented evidence that the loan is being serviced properly, which can be favorable in the eyes of underwriters when the seller is applying for a new loan.

**Seasoning the Loan:**

- Regular, documented payments over a certain period (like 12 months) can effectively "season" the loan.

- This history of timely payments can strengthen the seller's position when seeking a new loan, providing reassurance to lenders about the seller's financial responsibility.

Another major concern for sellers in subject-to real estate transactions is the potential failure of the buyer to make mortgage payments. This fear is rooted in the risk of financial and legal complications that the seller might face if the buyer defaults on the mortgage payments.

## Solution: Payment Failure Concerns

**Performance Clause in Agreement:**

- **Security Through Contractual Terms:** To alleviate the seller's fears, a performance clause is included in the agreement. This clause stipulates that if the buyer (in this case, me) fails to make payments, the property will automatically revert back to the seller, negating the need for a foreclosure process.

- **Seller's Protection:** This clause is crafted to provide maximum protection to the seller, ensuring their interests are safeguarded in the event of non-payment.

**Seller's Benefits in Case of Default:**

- **Financial Safeguards:** If the buyer defaults, the seller retains any down payment and all payments made thus far, along with any costs incurred for property improvements.

- **Financial Advantage:** Interestingly, in some scenarios, the seller might find themselves in a more advantageous financial position if the buyer defaults, as they keep the payments and regain the property.

**Reassuring the Seller:**

- **Demonstrating Reliability:** It's crucial to reassure the seller of the buyer's reliability. This can be done by showcasing the buyer's (my) consistent payment history and explaining the management and documentation of payments.

- **Use of a Licensed Loan Servicing Company:** Employing a company like West Star for managing subject-to loan payments can ensure transparency and reliability in the transaction process.

## Email Notifications for Peace of Mind:

- **Continuous Communication:** The seller receives email notifications for every mortgage payment made. This constant update serves as reassurance that the mortgage is being managed correctly.

- **Involving Key Stakeholders:** Notifications are also sent to the bank and the insurance company, ensuring all parties are informed.

## Improving the Seller's Credit:

**Credit Benefits:** Regular, on-time payments made by the buyer can positively impact the seller's credit score. This turns a potential concern into an advantage for the seller.

## Chapter Summary:

Creative financing opens up a realm of possibilities, enabling you to achieve your desired sale price while providing flexibility on other terms of the deal. These strategies require a clear understanding of your financial goals, the buyer's capabilities, and the market conditions. By leveraging these creative approaches, you can transform potential obstacles into mutually beneficial opportunities, ensuring that your real estate transactions are not only successful but also tailored to meet the unique needs of all parties involved.

Understanding and addressing the main objections to subject-to deals is crucial for ensuring a smooth and secure transaction for both sellers and buyers. Concerns about the debt-to-income ratio can be mitigated through strategies such as lease agreements, upfront payments, and the use of licensed loan servicing companies. These approaches help maintain the seller's financial standing and facilitate smoother transactions. Additionally, addressing potential

payment failure concerns is essential. Incorporating legal safeguards like performance clauses, using licensed loan servicing companies for transparent payment management, and providing regular updates to all parties involved can significantly boost the seller's confidence in the arrangement. By combining these financial and legal strategies, sellers are not only protected but also stand to improve their financial situation, turning potential risks into opportunities for long-term stability and credit enhancement. This comprehensive approach ensures peace of mind and fosters trust, making subject-to deals a viable and attractive option in real estate transactions.

*Chapter: 7*

# THE TRADITIONAL LISTING APPROACH

If you find that alternative selling methods don't align with your needs, the traditional way of selling your home remains a reliable and familiar choice. This approach, often the go-to method in real estate, involves a comprehensive process that, while time-intensive, can maximize your property's market value. We'll guide you through this well-trodden path, from listing your property to closing the sale, ensuring you navigate each step with confidence and clarity.

## Preparing Your Property for the Market

**In-Depth Market Analysis:** Start with a comprehensive analysis of current market trends. Understanding the local real estate climate, including prices of recently sold similar properties, helps in setting a competitive yet realistic price.

**Home Inspection:** Conduct a pre-listing home inspection. This step, often overlooked, can save you from surprises during the buyer's inspection. Addressing issues beforehand can prevent potential deal-breakers.

**Enhanced Curb Appeal:** Enhancing curb appeal goes beyond basic landscaping. Consider investing in minor exterior upgrades like new mailbox, house numbers, or even a fresh coat of paint on the front door.

**Interior Optimization:** Inside, focus on creating a universally appealing space. This might include repainting rooms with bold colors to more neutral tones, updating outdated light fixtures, or refinishing hardwood floors.

**Professional Home Staging:** Engage a professional stager to elevate the presentation of your home. Stagers understand how to highlight your home's strengths and downplay its weaknesses, making it appeal to the broadest audience.

**Energy Efficiency Upgrades:** Small upgrades like LED lighting, programmable thermostats, or improved insulation can be selling points, especially among environmentally-conscious buyers.

## Navigating the Traditional Sale Process

**Strategic Marketing Plan:** Develop a comprehensive marketing plan with your agent. This should include high-quality photography, a compelling property description, and leveraging various advertising channels, including digital and traditional media.

**Effective Online Presence:** Ensure your listing has a strong online presence. Most buyers start their search online, so your listing should be on all major real estate platforms, complete with virtual tours and floor plans.

**Open Houses and Private Showings:** Plan for multiple open houses and private showings. Flexibility is key here, as more showings typically lead to more offers.

**Skillful Negotiations:** Be prepared for multiple rounds of negotiations. This phase requires patience and skill to ensure you get the best deal without jeopardizing the sale.

**Handling Contingencies and Closing:** Be aware of various contingencies that buyers might include in their offers, such as financing or selling their current home. Navigating these effectively is crucial to moving towards a successful closing.

**Closing the Sale:** The final step involves a lot of paperwork and legal formalities. Work closely with your agent and a real estate attorney to ensure all documents are in order, and the closing process runs smoothly.

## Chapter Summary:

While this approach demands significant time and effort, the potential to maximize your property's sale price is unmatched. Leveraging my extensive experience, I guide my clients through each step, ensuring they not only achieve the best possible sale price but also understand and are comfortable with each phase of the process.

Chapter: 8

# YOUR PARTNER IN REAL ESTATE SOLUTIONS

## Our Commitment to Win-Win Solutions

Real estate transactions, particularly in stressful situations, can feel daunting and one-sided. However, my approach is fundamentally different. With 20+ years of experience in the industry, I have always prioritized creating solutions that are mutually beneficial. This win-win philosophy is the cornerstone of my practice.

## Understanding Mutual Benefit

The core of a win-win solution lies in understanding and respecting your needs as a property seller. Whether you are dealing with financial distress, managing an inherited property, or looking to offload a problematic rental, my goal is to find a resolution that alleviates your burden while offering fair value for your property. This approach ensures that you walk away from the transaction feeling relieved and satisfied.

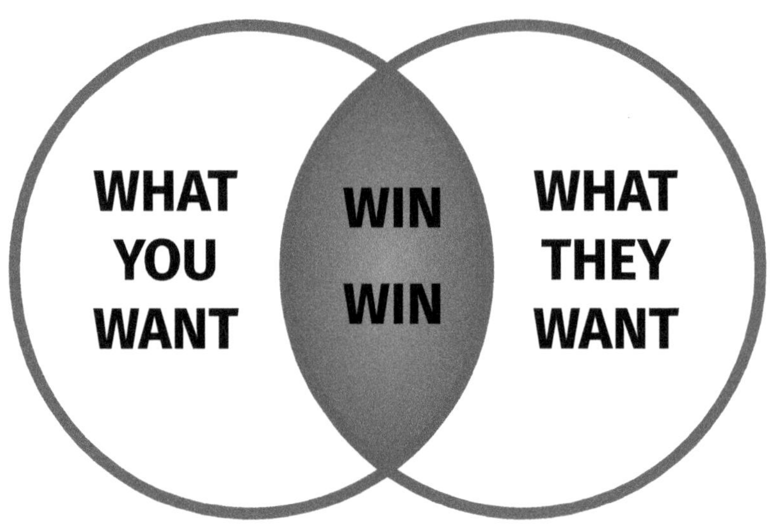

## Flexibility and Adaptability

Each client's situation is unique, and so are the solutions I offer. By being flexible and adaptable, I tailor my services to fit your specific circumstances. This might mean offering a quick cash sale for those in urgent need or providing creative financing solutions for more complex scenarios.

## Our Experience and Your Advantage

Over my 20+-year career, I have honed my skills in various facets of real estate, including investing, property management, and leading sales teams. This breadth of experience is not just a testament to my knowledge but a direct advantage to you.

## A Rich Network of Resources

My extensive network, encompassing top real estate professionals in the U.S. and Canada, is at your disposal. This network means access to a wealth of knowledge, diverse investment opportunities, and a vast market for your property.

## Proven Track Record in Problem Solving

Managing online leads and training sales professionals has equipped me with a unique perspective on real estate transactions. This experience has been instrumental in developing innovative problem-solving strategies, ensuring that no matter how complex your situation might seem, there is a solution available.

## Chapter Summary:

As your partner in real estate solutions, my commitment extends beyond mere transactions. It's about building relationships based on trust, respect, and a genuine desire to help. With my expertise, experience, and empathetic approach, I am not just a real estate professional; I am your ally in navigating through challenging times.

In the next chapter, we will explore real stories of success, illustrating how these principles have positively impacted the lives of sellers just like you.

*Chapter: 9*

# REAL STORIES, REAL SUCCESS

**Case Study #1: Inheriting Challenges, Discovering Solutions**

**Background:**

Sarah, a busy professional living in New York, unexpectedly inherited a house in Texas from her late father. The property, neglected for years, required significant repairs. Overwhelmed with the distance, time constraints, and financial implications of refurbishing it, Sarah felt trapped.

**Our Intervention:**

Upon contacting us, we quickly assessed the property and presented Sarah with a fair, no-obligation cash offer. Recognizing her situation, we ensured a rapid closing process, sparing her the burden of repairs or additional expenses.

## Outcome:

Sarah sold the house within weeks, relieved from the responsibilities of a distant, deteriorating property. This fast, hassle-free process allowed her to focus on her career and personal life without the added stress of managing an unwanted inheritance.

### Case Study #2: Financial Distress to Financial Relief

## Background:

John, grappling with financial challenges, faced the daunting prospect of bringing cash to the table at closing due to low equity in his home. The stress of potential foreclosure loomed over him, complicating his already precarious financial situation.

## Our Solution:

We stepped in to negotiate a seller financing arrangement suitable for a buy-and-hold investor. This strategy not only prevented the need for John to pay at closing but also ensured he received some cash for his immediate needs.

## Outcome:

John successfully closed the deal, averting the risk of foreclosure. He left the closing table with cash in hand, a substantial relief amidst his financial hardships. This solution provided him the necessary breathing room to reorganize his finances and move forward.

### Case Study #3: Simplifying the Move to Family

## Background:

Emily, a retired teacher, yearned to move closer to her grandchildren but dreaded the hassles of real estate transactions. The thought of dealing with agents, managing repairs, and enduring endless showings was overwhelming for her.

## Our Approach:

Recognizing Emily's desire for a straightforward process, we offered to purchase her property directly for cash. This proposal eliminated the need for repairs, realtors, or showings, aligning perfectly with her wish for simplicity and speed.

## Outcome:

Emily sold her property effortlessly, quickly relocating to be near her family. The swift, uncomplicated transaction allowed her to start her new life chapter without delay, surrounded by her loved ones. Her dream of being close to her grandchildren was realized sooner and with far less stress than she anticipated.

Each of these stories exemplifies our commitment to understanding and addressing unique seller circumstances. Through tailored solutions, we guide our clients towards positive outcomes, reinforcing our role as empathetic, skilled problem solvers in the real estate world.

# TAKING THE NEXT STEPS

## Contact Information

At the end of this journey, the path to resolution and peace of mind in your real estate challenges is clear. To take the next step, I invite you to reach out directly. Here's how you can contact me:

- Phone Number: 832-819-5496

- Email Address: josh@CashOutProperty.com

## Visit Our Website

For more detailed information about our services, client testimonials, and a comprehensive FAQ section, visit our website at www.CashOutProperty.com. Our site is designed to be user-friendly, providing you with a wealth of resources at your fingertips.

## Calling for Immediate Assistance

If you're in a situation that requires immediate attention, don't hesitate to call us. We understand the urgency that comes with personal emergencies, distressed properties, and other time-sensitive real estate issues.

## FAQs and Additional Resources

To assist you further, here's a list of frequently asked questions and additional resources:

## What makes a cash offer different from a traditional sale?

A cash offer provides a quick, hassle-free sale without the need for repairs or waiting for buyer financing.

## How fast can a sale be closed?

Typically, we can close sales much faster than traditional methods, often within days or weeks, depending on your specific situation.

## What if my property needs significant repairs?

We specialize in purchasing properties as-is, meaning you don't need to invest in repairs or upgrades before selling.

## Can you help with inherited properties?

Absolutely, we have extensive experience dealing with the unique challenges of inherited properties.

## Is there an obligation to accept an offer?

No, our consultation and offer come with no obligation. Our goal is to present you with the best solutions for your situation.

## What are the fees or commissions involved in your services?

Our service model prioritizes transparency and fairness. Unlike traditional real estate transactions, we do not charge any commissions or fees when purchasing your property directly.

## How do you determine the value of a property?

Property valuation is conducted through a comprehensive process that considers current market trends, the property's condition, location, and unique features. We aim to provide a fair and competitive offer that reflects the true value of your property.

## Can I sell my property if it's in foreclosure or has legal issues?

Yes, we specialize in dealing with properties facing legal challenges, including foreclosure. Our expertise allows us to navigate these complexities and still offer a viable solution to sell your property.

## What happens if my property is in a less-than-ideal location?

We assess properties on a case-by-case basis, and a less-than-ideal location does not automatically disqualify a property from being considered. We strive to find creative solutions that benefit both parties, regardless of location.

## How confidential is the sale process?

Confidentiality and privacy are core to our operations. All discussions, transactions, and personal information are handled with the utmost discretion and confidentiality.

## What if I need more time to move out after selling?

We offer flexible move-out options. If you need additional time after the sale, we can arrange a suitable timeline that allows for a comfortable transition to your new situation.

**Do you work with properties that have tenants?**

Yes, we work with properties that currently have tenants. We handle these situations delicately, ensuring legal compliance and fair treatment for all parties involved.

**How does the process differ for selling inherited properties?**

Selling an inherited property involves unique legal and emotional considerations. We guide you through the probate process, if applicable, and provide support and advice tailored to the nuances of inherited property sales.

**What makes your service different from traditional real estate agents?**

Our service differs in several ways: we offer direct purchasing, which eliminates many of the hassles and delays of traditional sales; there are no commissions or fees; we buy properties in 'as-is' condition; and we specialize in complex situations like foreclosures or inherited properties.

**Chapter Summary:**

In this chapter, we've provided several ways for you to take the next step towards solving your real estate challenges. Whether it's through a direct phone call, a visit to our website, or by seeking immediate assistance, my team and I are here to support you.

Remember, my approach is rooted in empathy, understanding, and a deep commitment to finding win-win solutions. Your journey towards a stress-free resolution starts with a simple step: reaching out to us. Let's embark on this journey together.

*Chapter: 11*

# CONCLUSION

### A Recap of How We Can Help

As we conclude this guide, let's revisit the key points that outline how we can assist you in navigating the challenges of real estate selling under distressing circumstances:

**Empathetic Understanding:** Recognizing your unique situation, whether it's financial distress, the complexities of inherited properties, or the urgency in a divorce settlement, my approach starts with empathy and understanding.

**Tailored Solutions:** Offering a range of solutions, from fast cash sales to creative financing, I ensure that your needs are met with the most suitable approach. Each solution is designed to offer relief, convenience, and a fair outcome.

**Ease and Convenience:** My processes are streamlined to remove the burden from your shoulders. With quick closings, no need for repairs, and handling all the paperwork, my focus is on making your experience as stress-free as possible.

**Professional Expertise:** Leveraging my 20+ years of experience in real estate, I bring a depth of knowledge and a proven track record in providing effective solutions to a myriad of real estate challenges.

**Commitment to Win-Win Outcomes:** At the heart of my philosophy is the belief in creating solutions that benefit all parties involved. Your satisfaction and peace of mind are paramount in every transaction.

## Inviting Your Journey with Us

Now that you have a deeper understanding of how we can assist you, I invite you to begin your journey with us. Whether you are ready to move forward with selling your property or still have questions, my team and I are here to guide you every step of the way.

Remember, you are not alone in this. Many have faced similar challenges and found relief and success through our services. Your situation, no matter how daunting it may seem, has a solution, and we are here to help you find it.

# FINAL THOUGHTS

This book is not just a guide but a testament to my commitment to helping individuals like you navigate the complex world of real estate under challenging circumstances. My hope is that it has provided you with valuable insights and a clear path forward.

As you close this book, know that the door to a new beginning is just a conversation away. I look forward to the opportunity to work with you and to be a part of your journey towards a successful and stress-free resolution.

Thank you for taking the time to read this guide, and I eagerly await the chance to connect with you soon.

# ONE LAST MESSAGE TO YOU

As you turn the final pages of this book, I want to take a moment to extend my sincerest congratulations to you. In choosing to invest your time in educating yourself, you've taken a significant and commendable step. Whether you're navigating personal challenges, exploring options for a property you own, or simply seeking knowledge, this journey of learning is a powerful testament to your commitment to making informed decisions.

The world of real estate, particularly in the context of the unique situations we've explored, can be complex and daunting. Yet, by seeking understanding, you're empowering yourself to face these challenges with confidence and clarity. Remember, knowledge is more than just power—it's the key to unlocking opportunities, overcoming obstacles, and paving the way for a brighter future.

I hope this book has provided you with valuable insights and a clearer perspective on the options available to you. More than that, I hope it has inspired you to believe in the possibility of positive outcomes, even in the most challenging circumstances.

As you move forward, I encourage you to carry the lessons and insights you've gained with you. And remember, you're not alone on this journey. If you ever find yourself seeking further guidance, needing a sounding board, or simply wishing to discuss your unique situation, don't hesitate to reach out.

Thank you for taking this journey with me. Here's to your continued growth, understanding, and success in all your real estate endeavors.

Wishing you all the best,

**Josh Cunningham**

# SPECIAL FREE BONUS GIFT FOR YOU

**Free Consultation Invitation for "Real Estate Solutions with Josh Cunningham"**

Discover Your Property's Potential: Free, No-Obligation Consultation

**You're Not Alone in This Journey**

Navigating the complexities of real estate can be overwhelming, especially when faced with personal challenges or unique property situations. Whether you're dealing with financial distress, managing an inherited property, or simply seeking a quick and hassle-free sale, I understand the myriad of emotions and decisions you're grappling with.

**Tailored Solutions, Just for You**

Each property, like its owner, has a unique story. That's why I offer personalized consultations, free of charge and without obligation. In our one-on-one session, we'll explore your specific situation, address your concerns, and evaluate your property's potential. You'll gain insights into the current market and learn what your home could truly be worth.

**Why Choose Josh Cunningham?**

- **20+ Years of Diverse Real Estate Experience:** From investing to property management, I've seen it all.

- **Win-Win Philosophy:** My commitment is to find solutions that benefit everyone involved.

- **Proven Track Record:** Trusted by top real estate owners across the U.S. and Canada.

- **Solution-Oriented Approach:** No matter how complex your situation, I am dedicated to finding the best outcome for you.

**Your Next Step**

Ready to discover what your home could be worth and explore your options? Schedule your free consultation today. Let's find the right solution together, with no pressure and no strings attached.

*Your property has potential. Let's unlock it together.*

**Contact Information**

- **Phone Number:** 832-819-5496

- **Email Address:** josh@CashOutProperty.com

- **Website:** www.CashOutProperty.com

# JOSH CUNNINGHAM

Growing up amidst the excitement and innovation of the dotcom boom, Josh Cunningham developed an insatiable desire to create something groundbreaking. This spirit led him to pursue a degree in Entrepreneurial Business Management from Texas A&M University, where he laid the foundation for a successful career as a visionary entrepreneur.

Josh's journey into the world of real estate began when he partnered with Frank Klesitz, the Founder and CEO of Vyral Marketing. Together, they traversed the country, attending every real estate seminar and mastermind event they could find. Through this experience, Josh identified the glaring need for a comprehensive, turnkey Inside Sales Assistant solution within the industry.

In 2013, with a keen sense of purpose and an unwavering drive for innovation, Josh founded rokrbox. Since its inception, the company has grown exponentially, handling over 3 million internet leads, employing 400 Inside Sales Assistants, and generating hundreds of millions in closed real estate sales.

However, Josh's success reaches far beyond the realm of real estate. Recognizing the importance of a thriving company culture, he fostered an environment that attracted top talent and nurtured their growth. This focus on culture not only propelled rokrbox to new heights but also allowed Josh the personal and business freedom to live in sunny San Diego and explore the country in an RV with his beloved wife and children.

Today, Josh Cunningham is highly sought after for his expertise in real estate, as well as his unique insights on building a company culture that creates massive profits. As a true testament to his entrepreneurial spirit, Josh continues to break boundaries, inspire others, and redefine what it means to be an innovative leader.

9 798330 369874